FANTASTIC VOYAGE: A POEM

FANTASTIC VOYAGE

ISBN: 978-1-960451-17-0

First paperback edition published by Stalking Horse Press, May 2025

www.stalkinghorsepress.com

Design by James Reich

Stalking Horse Press

Santa Fe, New Mexico

PRAISE FOR MATT BIALER

"Who else but Matt Bialer could make a poem filled with Brontosauruses, New Coke, finding old footage of your girlfriend on YouTube, creamed spinach and sex ed filmstrips and somehow juggle all of this (and more!) so casually that you don't notice that he's breaking your heart until he has. Bialer is unabashedly direct and clear, in the best way; in the minutiae of his life you will see the reflection of your own."

> —Matthew Rohrer, author of *The Sky Contains the Plans*
> and *The Others*

"*Matrix* is a deeply moving poem of loss and reconstruction. Matt Bialer is a master of concision and evocation, bringing an incredible palette of nuances to often contradictory feelings. A must-read for all lovers of real-life, raw and beautiful poetry."

> —Seb Doubinsky, author of *Missing Signal*
> and *The Song of Synth*

"In *Matrix*, Bialer's 60th birthday thrusts him into a poetic contemplation on both the striking brevity of life as well as the enduring nature of memory. The readers take a journey moving back and forth through time and the ever-changing landscape of dinosaurs, 35 mml film, vinyl records, and other extinct or obsolete objects and beings. Only an 82-million-year-old tooth, set in a matrix of stone, survives like "a footprint across time." The poignancy of grief for his beloved wife's passing, and the hopefulness of a new love are vivid reminders that although life is ephemeral, the human capacity to love is undying."

> —Loretta Oleck, author of *Paper Chains*
> and *Songs from the Black Hole*

FANTASTIC VOYAGE

MATT BIALER

STALKING HORSE PRESS
SANTA FE, NEW MEXICO

the moon was full last night: today, low tide was low:
black shoals of mussels exposed to the risk
of air
and, earlier, of sun,
waved in and out with the waterline, waterline inexact,
caught always in the event of change:

From "Corsons Inlet" by A. R. Ammons

This book is dedicated to my honey, Mary Kathleen Flynn.

FANTASTIC VOYAGE

I

When my wife
Lenora
Was fatally ill
Over a period
Of 14 years
I accompanied her
To the doctor
Many times

Many times

When we
Had to make
Critical decisions
About treatment
Or when things
Were taking
A turn
For the worse

A turn
For the worse

I started
To neglect
My own health needs

High blood pressure
High cholesterol

I stopped going
For annual physicals

Because I
Didn't need
More doctor visits

We had
Too many already

Too many

As an old
Favorite band
Humble Pie
Used to say:

I don't need
No doctor

"I don't need
No doctor
'Cause I know
What's ailing me
I don't need
No doctor
No, No
'Cause I know

What's ailing me
I've been
Too long
Away from my baby
Ah
I don't need
No doctor

I don't need
No doctor"

But I did

I did

My medical needs
Were silenced

Mute

So after
Lenora died
I asked
A cousin
Of hers
At a gathering
After her burial
What advice
Did she have
For me?

She lost
Her own husband
Years earlier

Don't make
Any big decisions
For at least
A year
And take care
Of yourself

Take care
Of yourself

My medical needs
Were silenced

Mute

And so
I started
Seeing a new doctor

Not my old one
In Hell's Kitchen
By Times Square

But close
To me:
Park Slope
In Brooklyn

So it would
Be easier
So I would
Be motivated

My medical needs
Were silenced

Mute

My new doctor
Is a lot younger
Than my previous one

And she treated
My high blood pressure
And high cholesterol

I had told her
That Lenora died
From metastatic breast cancer

And that
I was
Still grieving

Still grieving

She asked me
How long ago
Did she pass?

At the time
It had been
Two years

She replied:
"Grief should
Only last
For a year"

What
I thought?

She looked
At me
Like I had
Another ailment
That needed
To be treated

Another ailment

Grief should
Only last
For a year

Yeah
Maybe for
A hamster
Or a goldfish

She clearly
Never lost
A partner
Or a parent
Or a child
Or friend
Or even
A dog or cat

I've been
Too long
Away from my baby
Ah
I don't need
No doctor

I don't need
No doctor
But I did
And I
Ignored her comment

Ignored her comment

She asked me
When was
The last time
I had
A colonoscopy?

When was
The last time?

I couldn't remember
Seemed recent
Maybe six years ago?

I had brain fog
From grief

It literally
Altered time
For me

Like she was
Still here

I was endlessly
Reliving
When she was alive

Endlessly

Caught in the web
Of a time tunnel

Like the 1960s
Irwin Allen TV show
I grew up on:
The Time Tunnel

American color
Science fiction TV series
Around a theme
Of time travel adventure

While conducting
An experiment
In time travel
Scientists Dr. Tony Newman
And Dr. Douglas Phillips
Find themselves
Whisked from
Time period
To time period
While their colleagues
Back in the present
Desperately struggle
To retrieve
The two men

The pair frequently
Find themselves
On the brink
Of a major historical event

And while
The scientists
Back home
Can see
The action unfolding
Wherever Newman
And Phillips are
They are helpless
To offer any aid

Helpless

Around a theme
Of time travel

I am both
Newman and Phillips
And their colleagues
Back in the present

Helpless
To offer any aid

Helpless

I had brain fog
From grief

It literally
Altered time
For me

Like she was
Still here

I was endlessly
Reliving
When she was alive
Endlessly
Caught in the web
Of a time tunnel
A few years later
Time is righting itself

Righting itself

Steadying

So a few months ago
I realized
That it was
Ten years ago

When I turned 50

That I got
My first
And only colonoscopy

So I'm due

I'm due

At my annual physical
After the first
Of the year
I tell my doctor
That I was mistaken

I'm due

She sends
A referral
To Mount Sinai Medical Center
Upper West Side Endoscopy Center
That very day
I get a call
From them
To schedule
An appointment

They send
Diet and
Medication restrictions

The guck
I have to drink

"By New York State regulations
A companion
(Adult 18 years
Or older)
Must be available
To accompany you home
After the procedure
Since the sedation
You receive
May impair
Your reflexes
And judgement"

Ten years ago
Lenora picked me up

Now she obviously can't

I ask my girlfriend
Of almost four years
Mary
If she will pick me up
"Of course
I will
Let me send you
Some available dates"

So sweet
Of her

She'll pick me up
On the Upper West Side
And take me
In an Uber
To my house in Brooklyn

Time travel

I never
Would have known
That ten years later
I have a girlfriend

I schedule it
For a Friday

And it's coming up

Coming up

Next week

But this weekend
Mary
And her daughter
Samantha
Who is 21
Like my daughter Izzy
And some friends
Will see a revival
Of the musical
Once Upon a Mattress

Colonoscopy

Is a procedure
That lets
Your health care provider
Check the inside
Of your entire colon

Large intestine

Procedure is done
Using a long
Flexible tube
Called a colonoscope

The tube
Has a light
And a tiny camera
On one end

Travels through
The U-shaped tunnel
That is my large intestine

A spy camera

During the procedure
Your provider
May remove tissue
Or polyps
Abnormal growth
For further examination

Polyps

I think
Of polyps underwater

And anemones
And jellyfish

Coral reefs

Rainforests
Of the ocean

Polyps

Soft corals

In the *phylum*
Cnidaria
From the Greek word
Meaning stinging needles

Tentacles

Polyps

Soft corals
Have silky bodies
That can move
And flow
With the ocean currents

Move
And flow
With the ocean currents

Resemble plants
Of trees with limbs
Blowing in the wind

In soft corals
Polyps create
Small
Pointy structures
Called sclerites
That help them
Keep their shape

A colony of polyps
Actually act
As one organism

One organism

The tube
Has a light
And a tiny camera
On one end
Travels through
A U-shaped tunnel
That is my large intestine

A spy camera
I had brain fog
From grief

It literally
Altered time
For me

Caught in the web
Of a time tunnel

Helpless
To offer any aid

Helpless

Grief should
Only last
For a year

I don't need
No doctor

Polyps

Tentacles

That can move
And flow
With the ocean currents

Move
And flow
With the ocean currents

Rainforests
Of the ocean
Act
As one organism

One organism

A voyage
To the bottom
Of the sea

||

The tube
Has a light
And a tiny camera
On one end
Travels through
A U-shaped tunnel
That is my large intestine

A spy camera

Ten years later
Mary
Will pick me up
Instead of
Lenora

Mary
Will pick me up

Abnormal growth
For further examination

Polyps

I think
Of polyps underwater
Tentacles

And anemones
And jellyfish

Coral reefs

Rainforests
Of the ocean

Mary
Will pick me up

Time tunnel

The Irwin Allen show
The Time Tunnel

Makes me
Think of
Another 1960s
Irwin Allen show

Voyage
to the Bottom
of the Sea

A 1964-1968
American science fiction
Television series
Based on the
1961 film
Of the same name
Both were created
By Irwin Allen
Which also used
The film's sets
Costumes
Props
Special effects models
And even footage

The pilot episode
"Eleven Days to Zero"
Introduces the futuristic
Nuclear submarine
S.S.R.V
Seaview
And the lead members
Of her crew
Including the designer
And builder
Of the vessel
Admiral Harriman Nelson
And Commander Lee Crane
Who becomes
The *Seaview*'s captain
After the murder
Of her original
Commanding officer

The submarine
Is based
At the Nelson Institute
Of Marin Research
In Santa Barbara
California
And is often moored
500 feet
Beneath the facility
In a secret underground
Submarine pen
Carved out of
Solid rock

The *Seaview*
Is officially
The undersea marine research
And visits
Many exotic locations
In the Seven Seas

But its secret mission
Is to defend the planet
From all world
And extraterrestrial threats
In the then future
Of the 1970s

Defend the planet

The first season's
31 episodes
Included gritty
Atmospheric story lines
Devoted to

The Cold War themes
Including espionage
And fantastical elements:

Aliens
Sea monsters
And dinosaurs
Were featured
But the primary villains
Were hostile foreign governments

The *Seaview*
Stealthily glides
Among the sea grasses

Coral reefs

Rainforests
Of the ocean

Polyps

Soft corals

In the *phylum*
Cnidaria
From the Greek word
Meaning stinging needles

Tentacles

Polyps

Soft corals
Have silky bodies

That can move
And flow
With the ocean currents

Move
And flow
With the ocean currents

Resemble plants
Of trees with limbs
Blowing in the wind
In soft corals
Polyps create
Small
Pointy structures
Called sclerites
That help them
Keep their shape

A colony of polyps
Actually act
As one organism

One organism

The tube
Has a light
And a tiny camera
On one end
Travels through
A U-shaped tunnel
That is my large intestine

A spy camera

I had brain fog
From grief

It literally
Altered time
For me
Caught in the web
Of a time tunnel

Helpless
To offer any aid

Helpless

Grief should
Only last
For a year

I don't need
No doctor

The first episodes began
With Admiral Nelson
And the crew
Of the *Seaview*
Fighting against
A foreign government
To prevent
A world-threatening earthquake

And continuing with
A foreign government
Destroying American submarines
With new technologies
In "The Fear Makers"

And "The Enemies"

"The Price of Doom"
A scientist
On a research facility
In Antarctica discovers
A new form
Of sea plankton
That turns monstrously large

"Turn Back the Clock"
A lone survivor
Of a doomed Antarctic expedition
Is rescued
The *Seaview* takes him
To see
If there really is
A dinosaur laden
Tropical paradise
Somewhere
In the Antarctic

"Hot Line"
A Soviet rocket
Carrying a satellite
Is crashing back
To Earth
And the *Seaview*
Must transport
Two Russian missile experts
To find and disarm it

"The Invaders"
An undersea earthquake
Exhumes hundreds

Of strange metallic capsules
And a peaceful humanoid creature
Who could
Destroy mankind
Is restored
To life
After millions
Of years
In suspended animation

"Mutiny"
An attack
By a giant jellyfish
An attack
By a giant jellyfish

A new form
Of sea plankton
That turns monstrously large

The tube
Has a light
And a tiny camera
On one end
Travels through
A U-shaped tunnel
That is my large intestine

A spy camera

Ten years later
Mary
Will pick me up
Instead of
Lenora

Mary
Will pick me up

Abnormal growth
For further examination
Polyps

I think
Of polyps underwater

Tentacles

And anemones
And jellyfish

Coral reefs

Rainforests
Of the ocean

Mary
Will pick me up

The Time Tunnel

*Voyage
to the Bottom
of the Sea*

The *Seaview*
Stealthily glides

Among the sea grasses

Coral reefs

Rainforests
Of the ocean

"Eleven days to zero
In the mists of silence
The sky is falling
Into the cradle of the deep

I am not what I am
There's a double
An imposter
Not me
Admiral Nelson
Can't you see?
Time is out of joint
Under sea
Reality
Nothin' above us
Below us only sea
It's crash dive
To the bottom
Of the sea....

Eleven days to zero
In the mists of silence
The sky is falling
Into the cradle of the deep
The shadow man from the depths
Voyage to
the Bottom
of the Sea"

I meet Mary
And Samantha
And Mary's close friend
Ann
And Gillian
And Gillian's friend
Kara
At City Center
In midtown Manhattan
For a matinee
Revival performance
Of the musical comedy
Once Upon a Mattress

Once Upon a Mattress

A musical comedy
With music by Mary Rodgers
Lyrics by Marshall Barer
And a book by
Jay Thompson
Dean Fuller
And Marshall Barer

It opened
Off-Broadway
In May 1959
And then moved
To Broadway

The play
Was written
As a humorous adaption
Of the 1835
Hans Christian Anderson fairy tale
The Princess and the Pea

Once Upon a Mattress
Marked the Broadway debut
Of the brilliant comedian
Carol Burnett
Who originated the role
Of Princess Winnifred

It was also adapted
For television
Three times:
1964
1972
And 2005
With Carol Burnett
In all three productions

In the last one
Burnett played
The evil Queen Aggravin
Mother of Prince Dauntless

I think that
I might be
The only one
In our crew
Who has never seen it before
In any form

In this version
Sutton Foster
Takes on the role
Of Princess Winnifred
Apparently with the blessing
Of Carol Burnett herself

The Queen
Has made sure
That thirteen princesses
Have already failed
Their tests
To become the bride
Of the bumbling Prince Dauntless
Not the sharpest sword
In the castle
But still smart enough
To become endearingly smitten
With a brash and unrefined
Princess Winnifred
Who goes by Fred
Fred
Literally emerges
From the swamp
And swims the moat
To become the bride
Of Prince Dauntless
Endearingly played
By Michael Urie

Fred is described
By another character
As a "strangely energetic
Swamp girl"

That's about right

Urie and Foster
Are a great odd-duck pairing
He has extended
Monotone whines
And petulant stomps
Of his feet
While she goes for
Gangly tomboy swagger
After Fred emerges
From the swamp
And swims the moat
She pulls a raccoon
Out of her hair
And chucks leeches
From her back
Into the audience
Leeches

But Dauntless
Is in love

He's just as excited
By the leeches
As she is
And carries one
Around with him

I think
Of polyps underwater

Tentacles

And anemones
And jellyfish

Coral reefs

Rainforests
Of the ocean

Mary
Will pick me up
The Time Tunnel

Voyage
to the Bottom
of the Sea

The *Seaview*
Stealthily glides
Among the sea grasses

The Queen asks Fred:
"You swam the moat?"

She replies:
"Does she ever say anything else
Except 'You swam the moat?'"

The Queen thinks
She is no princess

No princess

But an imposter

An imposter

I am not what I am
There's a double
An imposter
Not me
Admiral Nelson
Can't you see?
Time is out of joint
Under sea
Reality
Nothin' above us
Below us only sea

"Do you mean to
Ask me
To believe
That you're a true princess
Of royal blood
And am I
To actually understand
That you have
The nerve
And the gall
And the presumption
To apply
For my son's hand
In marriage....

You are laboring
Under a very unfortunate
Misapprehension
My dear
My son isn't
Going to marry
A moat swimmer
Not while

I have breath
In my body"

Prince Dauntless
Tells his mother:
"You ought
To see her swim Mama
She's wonderful...

I like her Mama
She swam the moat"

She swam the moat

I take Mary's hand
During the show
Whisper to her:
"What fun this is
What a great find"
Fred sings
To Dauntless:

"I come
From the land
Of the foggy
Foggy dew
Ooh
Ooh
Ooh
Where walking
Through the meadow
In the morning
Is like walking
Through glue...

The swamps of home
Are brushed
With green and gold
At break of day
At break of day

The swamps of home
Are lovely to behold
From far away
From far away

In my soul
Is the beauty
Of the bog
In my memory
The magic of mud

I know that blood
Is thicker than water
But the swamps of home
Are thicker than blood…

Where e'er I roam
My heart
Grows dank
And cold
My face grows gray
When shadows fall
And I hear
The call
Of the swamps
Of home…

I hear it
Calling me now….

Listen to the voice
Of the swamp"

When the show
Is over
We all applaud
I have this sudden thought
I do a double-take

A pinch-myself moment

I forgot
It's ten years later

That I am now with Mary

I am in the time tunnel
Helpless
To offer any aid

Helpless

I had brain fog
From grief

It literally
Altered time
For me

Like she was
Still here

I was endlessly
Reliving
When she was alive

Endlessly

Caught in the web
Of a time tunnel

She'll pick me up
On the Upper West Side
And take me
In an Uber
To my house in Brooklyn

Time tunnel

I never
Would have known
That ten years later
I have a girlfriend

Listen to the voice
Of the swamp

I hold Mary's hand
And squeeze it

Thankful for her
For her friends
And family

Thankful for Samantha

I think about
How grief has been
A swamp

A moat

In my soul
Is the beauty
Of the bog

And how
I swam
Across them

To be with her

In the here
And now

Can't you see?
Time is out of joint
Under sea
Reality
Nothin' above us
Below us only sea
It's crash dive
To the bottom
Of the sea....

Eleven days to zero
In the mists of silence
The sky is falling
Into the cradle of the deep
The shadow man from the depths
Voyage to
the Bottom
of the Sea

In my soul
Is the beauty
Of the bog

In my memory
The magic of mud

IV

It's Thursday
The day before
My colonoscopy

Once Upon a Colonoscopy

I can only eat
Real foods
Until 11:30 am today
And I just did
I had an egg sandwich

I read over
All of the "rules"
That Mount Sinai
E-mailed me:

"If you do not
Have an escort
Your procedure
Will be canceled"

Ten years later
Mary
Will pick me up
Instead of
Lenora

Mary
Will pick me up

The Time Tunnel

*Voyage
to the Bottom
of the Sea*

She'll pick me up
On the Upper West Side
And take me
In an Uber
To my house in Brooklyn

Time tunnel

I never
Would have known
That ten years later
I have a girlfriend

Listen to the voice
Of the swamp

Can have clear fluids
Up to 3 hours prior
To the procedure

Nothing to drink
Three hours before

Nothing to drink

Otherwise clear broth
Apple juice
Tea with no milk

Then later today
I start to drink
The guck
The guck

I feel like
I am in prison

Or on jury duty

You have to be there
It's against the law to leave
This is the jury duty
Of the body

Of the body

I just want
To get it over with

Get it over with

I go on Facebook
And see
That a widow friend

Has a downed tree
In her yard
With a photo
And a comment:
"Just what I need"

People comment
That at least
It didn't hit the house

True
She also
Has realtors
Calling her
About that house
No doubt
Because they
Read the obituaries

I've been
Through all that too

Realtors leaving
Notes on my door

"I hear you've had
A change in your life"

A change in your life

And I've had to deal with
By myself
Floods in our finished basement
Furnaces breaking down
Two new toilets

New dishwasher
A leak from the ceiling

Grief is a downed tree
That hit the house

A gargantuan tree

An attack
By a giant jellyfish

Tentacles

Aliens
Sea monsters
And dinosaurs

It's been
A few years now

But I plan
To sell my house

Too many memories

Too hard to upkeep
By myself

I will move
To the Upper East Side
To be near Mary

Izzy has signed off
On it

She just said
Now while I'm in college

And she's about
To graduate

I'm swimming the moat

Listen to the voice
Of the swamp

I plan
To sell my house
Abort mission

Abandon ship

Abandon ship

Once Upon a Colonoscopy

Having one
Makes me think
Of the 1966
Science fiction film

Fantastic Voyage

Starring Stephen Boyd
Raquel Welch
Edmond O'Brien
Donald Pleasance

About a shrinking machine
Used to send

A mini submarine
Called *Proteus*
And its crew
Inside the body
And the bloodstream
Of a defecting scientist

During the Cold War
Both the United States
And the Soviet Union
Have discovered
The shrinking technology
Which is limited
In practicality
Because of how short-lived
The effect is

But the scientist
Jan Benes
Had discovered
How to overcome
The limit
And enemy agents
Will stop
At nothing
To prevent the secret
From escaping
From behind the Iron Curtain

Benes
Wounded in an attack
Is comatose
And dying from
An extremely inoperable blood clot
So the US miniaturization task force

Are shrunken
To remove the clot
From the inside
Of his brain

Remove the clot
From inside
Of his brain

Operating on it
At the cellular level

But they have
Sixty minutes
To complete the mission

Sixty minutes

Or they'll grow
Back to normal
While inside his body

To make matters
More dangerous
And dire
An enemy agent
Is trying to stop them

The protagonist
Charles Grant (Boyd)
Who smuggled
The scientist
From behind
The Iron Curtain
Has to make sure

The mission succeeds
While not knowing
Who he can trust
On the crew

They fight off
An attack
From white corpuscles
Caught in
A tornado-like storm
Inside the lungs

And many more obstacles

An undetected arteriovenous fistula
Forces them to detour
Through the heart
While cardiac arrest
Must be induced
To at best
Reduce turbulence
That would be
Strong enough
To destroy *Proteus*
The sub enters
The lymphatic system
But the reticular fibers
Start to interfere

The crew
Is then forced
To pass through
The inner ear
Requiring all outside personnel
To make no noise

To prevent devastating shocks

But while the crew
Is removing reticular fibers
Clogging *Proteus'* vents
And making the engine overheat
A fallen surgical tool
Causes the crew
To be thrown about
And Cora Peterson (Welch)
Is nearly killed
By antibodies

I think
Of polyps underwater

And anemones
And jellyfish

Coral reefs

Rainforests
Of the ocean

Polyps

Soft corals

In the *phylum*
Cnidaria
From the Greek word
Meaning stinging needles

Tentacles

Polyps

Soft corals
Have silky bodies
That can move
And flow
With the ocean currents

Move
And flow
With the ocean currents

Resemble plants
Of trees with limbs
Blowing in the wind
In soft corals
Polyps create
Small
Pointy structures
Called sclerites
That help them
Keep their shape

A colony of polyps
Actually act
As one organism

One organism

The tube
Has a light
And a tiny camera
On one end
Travels through
A U-shaped tunnel

That is my large intestine

A spy camera

I had brain fog
From grief

It literally
Altered time
For me

Caught in the web
Of a time tunnel

Helpless
To offer any aid

Helpless

Grief should
Only last
For a year

I don't need
No doctor
Polyps

Tentacles

That can move
And flow
With the ocean currents

Move
And flow

With the ocean currents

Rainforests
Of the ocean

Act
As one organism
One organism

A voyage
To the bottom
Of the sea

The crew are
Able to reboard Proteus
With only six minutes remaining
To operate
And exit the body

During the surgery
Is it revealed
That the enemy agent
Is Dr. Michaels (Pleasance)

He knocks out Owens
And takes control
Of the *Proteus*
While the crew
Is outside
For the operation

As Duval finished
Removing the clot
With a laser
Michaels tries

To crash the submarine
Into the same area
Of Benes' brain
To kill him

Kill him

Grant fired the laser
At the ship
Causing it
To veer away
And crash

Michaels is trapped
In the wreckage
With the controls
Pinning him
To his seat

Abort mission

Abandon ship

Abandon ship

He attracts the attention
Of the dreaded white blood cells
White blood cells

Account for
Only 1% of our blood
But their impact
Is huge

Also called Leukocytes

They protect us
Against illness and disease

They are
Always at war

Always at war
Flow through
Our bloodstream
To fight viruses
Bacteria
And other foreign invaders
When our bodies
Are in distress
And a particular area
Is under attack
White blood cells
Rush in
To help destroy
The harmful substance

White blood cells
Are made
In the bone marrow
Stored in our blood
And lymph tissues

Some white blood cells
Called neutrophils
Have a short life

Less than a day

Our bone marrow
Is always making them

When Lenora's
Breast cancer cells
Were in her bone marrow
She had trouble
Producing white blood cells

It was alarming

Transplants
Would only last
A day or two
The doctor aimed
A specific chemotherapy
At her bone marrow

It was a nightmare

A nightmare

There are
Five different kinds
Of white blood cells

Monocytes
Are the most common

Have longer lifespan

Lymphocytes create antibodies
To fight invaders

Dr. Michaels
Was a foreign invader

A harmful substance

And so
The white blood cells
Consume Michaels
And the ship

Consume
Giant blobs
All over *Proteus*

Consume
In the *phylum*
Cnidaria
From the Greek word
Meaning stinging needles

Tentacles

Polyps

The remaining crew
Quickly swim
To one of Benes' eyes

And escape
Through a tear duct

Rescued

Seconds before
They return
To normal size

Dr. Michaels
Being attacked
By the blobs

White corpuscles
Gave me nightmares
As kid

Nightmares

It's Thursday evening
And it's on
To the next phase
Of my own fantastic voyage
It's time to mix
And drink the guck

An entire 238 gram bottle
Of Miralax
With 64 ounces
Of lemon Gatorade

I drink half
Of the solution tonight
And the other half
At 5:30 am
In the morning

It's all
To clean out
My colon

It actually tastes better
Than it did 10 years ago

Someone tells me
That they've been trying
To refine the process

Another friend tells me
He has to go back again
Because his colon
Wasn't clear enough

Hope that's not me

Later
I take an Uber
To the Upper West Side
Endoscopy Center
Colonoscopy

Is a procedure
That lets
Your health care provider
Check the inside
Of your entire colon

Large intestine

Procedure is done
Using a long
Flexible tube
Called a colonoscope

The tube
Has a light
And a tiny camera
On one end

Travels through
The U-shaped tunnel
That is my large intestine

A spy camera

Can't you see?
Time is out of joint
Under sea
Reality
Nothin' above us
Below us only sea
It's crash dive
To the bottom
Of the sea...
Eleven days to zero
In the mists of silence
The sky is falling
Into the cradle of the deep
The shadow man from the depths

Voyage to
the Bottom
of the Sea

I don't need
No doctor

Polyps

Tentacles

That can move
And flow
With the ocean currents

Move
And flow
With the ocean currents

Rainforests
Of the ocean

Act
As one organism

One organism
A voyage
To the bottom
Of the sea

I arrive
And I lie
On a table
And they put me
On oxygen
And an IV
For fluids
And some sort
Of electrodes
For my chest

I joke and ask them
Are they turning me
Into Frankenstein's monster?

I receive MAC
Monitored Anesthesia Care

The same stuff
That killed Michael Jackson

I am told
I will be out
Within ten seconds

Next thing
I know
I wake up
In a recovery room

I don't remember
A thing

Not even a dream

I have gone through
A time tunnel

And I eventually
Walk out
To Mary
Who is waiting
For me
In the reception area

Ten years ago
Lenora picked me up

Now she obviously can't

I ask my girlfriend
Of almost four years
Mary
If she will pick me up

"Of course
I will
Let me send you
Some available dates"

So sweet
Of her

She'll pick me up
On the Upper West Side
And take me
In an Uber
To my house in Brooklyn

Time travel

I never
Would have known
That ten years later
I have a girlfriend

We get an Uber
And she takes me home
To Brooklyn

The curtain has come down
On Once Upon a Colonoscopy
I don't need
No doctor

"I don't need
No doctor
'Cause I know
What's ailing me
I don't need
No doctor
No, No
'Cause I know
What's ailing me
I've been

Too long
Away from my baby
Ah
I don't need
No doctor

I don't need
No doctor"

I swam the moat
The remaining crew
Quickly swim
To one of Benes' eyes

And escape
Through a tear duct

Rescued

Seconds before
They return
To normal size

I swam the moat

Rescued in a tear duct

On a fantastic voyage
With Mary

FANTASTIC VOYAGE

Matt Bialer is the author of over a dozen collections of poetry including *Always Say Goodnight* (KYSO Flash, 2020), *Maze* (Finishing Line Press, 2021), View-Master Land (Finishing Line Press 2023) and *Matrix* (Saint Julian Press, 2023). His poems have appeared in many print and online journals including *Retort, Le Zaporogue, Green Mountains Review, Gobbet, Forklift Ohio*, and *H_NGM_N*.

In addition, Matt is an acclaimed black and white street photographer who has exhibited his work widely. Some of his images are in the permanent collections of The Brooklyn Museum, The Museum of the City of New York, and The New York Public Library. He is also an accomplished watercolor landscape painter with work in many private collections.